For Rae Ann & Richard Schuster

Love & peace

Emeng R. Tang

鄧
和
平
神
父

CHINA
CONNECTION
Emery Tang

An American-born Chinese braids his life and ancestral strands into a unique journal.

A PILGRIMAGE book from
Resource Publications, Inc.
San Jose, California 95112

Photos by the author.
Brush paintings by Paul Kuo.
Book and jacket design by Ben Lizardi.

Editorial Director: Kenneth Guentert
Production Editor: Scott Alkire
Mechanical Layout: Agnes Hou

ISBN 0-89390-080-X
Library of Congress Catalog Card Number: 86-060169
Printed and bound in Hong Kong 5 4 3 2 1

Contents

With love and gratitude
to Snow Flower and Constant Abundance
and their children, my brothers and sisters,
whose lives intertwine with mine — forever:
Ah-ping
Mei-li
Ah-moy
Ah-yung
Ak-ah
Kwi-ah
Lok-ah
Ah-siu

—Ah-wo

Introduction
by Kenneth Guentert

Major travel, perhaps because I've done relatively little, has always been a kind of pilgrimage for me.

My first trip out of the country was to the Yucatan; I came home awed by the magnificence of the ruins that seemed everywhere to sprout from the soil and angered that my high-quality formal education had said nothing at all about this huge civilization buried under the rocks of my own continent.

My second trip was a two-week backpacking search for my grandfather's village in the Black Forest of Germany. I found it — and with it the strength to begin a journey into publishing on my own terms.

My third trip was a five-week adventure on an archeological dig in Capernaum, on the shore of the Sea of Galilee. We found a large horde of gold coins — for fun and Israel — and I found greater treasures. The Bible. The Land. The God of my ancestors. Home again.

As a traveler, a pilgrim, a searcher, I am hardly unique. True, some people — maybe even most — search for nothing deeper than the best seafood restaurant and come back with nothing more interesting than 100 snapshots of themselves, backsides attached to every monument and museum on their tour. But our American restlessness, seen in even the worst tourist, is a hunger for something. We travel for mystical reasons, the same reasons we walk along a beach or climb a mountain. God seems to rest in those magical places where one thing connects to another — where the water connects to the earth or where the sky connects to the earth or where our going out connects to our coming in.

Emery Tang, like most Americans, has the genes of a wanderer. He is also blessed with the Taoist (or is it Christian?) understanding that you only find by losing. That you go out to come in. And that you sprout wings to find roots. When I happened on a mimeographed journal of his 1984 trip to his ancestral homeland, the editor in me couldn't help but see a wonderful beginning for a line of "Pilgrimage Books" that would explore the connection between these journeys of the soul and journeys on the land. The photos, which do not include a single one of the author backed up against a monument, add to the pleasures of the road. Travel well.

Prologue

Once upon a time, early in this century, a fearless young man set sail eastward from the land of his fathers, The Central Kingdom (中國). His golden dream would one day become real in the land called Beautiful (美國) which lay many thousands of miles beyond the eastern horizon. There he was destined to meet and to marry a lovely bride who would bear him many children.

For wasn't the name given him at birth by the Family Tang Constant Abundance (鄧維盛)? And so it came to pass.

In the distant land called Beautiful, Snow Flower (余雪花) was born, the first of her race in a place that is called The Bird that Rises from its Ashes.

Constant Abundance and Snow Flower met. Their love united them and many children were born to them. There were four sons: Just Heart (心平), Peace (和平), Virtuous Principle (德平) and Tranquil Delight (樂平) — and five daughters: Beautiful One (美利), Pure Plum Blossom Moon (月梅), Lovely Forgiving Moon (月容), Noble Cassia Moon (月桂), and Graceful Elegant Moon (月秀).

* * *

All of which is to say that the young Tang Shing migrated to America from Canton, China in the early 1900's, met and married Lucy Yee Sing in Phoenix, Arizona. They had four sons: Thomas, Richard (Emery), Robert, Eugene — and five daughters: Mary, Margaret, Alice, Rose Marie and Patricia.

* * *

In the Year of the Rat, 4682, it came to pass that I, Peace, was the third member of the children of Constant Abundance and Snow Flower to travel to the land of our ancestors, Cathay, also known as The Central Kingdom or China. I had already been preceded by my brother Just Heart and my sister, Plum Blossom Moon.

* * *

All of which is to say that in 1984, I, Emery (Richard) was the third of Tang Shing and Lucy Yee Sing's children to visit what is now the People's Republic of China. Thomas and Margaret had been there before me.

* * *

''Are there any Franciscans around?'' I asked, hoping there would be a chance of meeting some.

The bishop's eyes shifted ever so slightly and tellingly. The memory of humiliations, imprisonments, dispersions and even executions of thousands of priests and religious by the Communist government for their resistance is a ghastly nightmare.

''No, there are none,'' he murmured softly. And we changed the subject.

6

Who Am I?

I was born at home — as were all my brothers and sisters — in August, 1927. There wasn't much I could do about the time and place — or anything, for that matter.

But because I was born in the Year of the Rabbit, Theodora Lau writes in her book, "Chinese Horoscopes":

> I am in tune with the
> Pulse of the universe.
> In my quiet and solitude
> I hear the melodies of the soul.
> I float above commonplace
> Dissent and decay.
> I subdue by my ability to conform.
> I color my word
> In delicate pastel hues.
> I epitomize harmony and inner peace.

Wow! Do I really believe all that? Hmmm.

And yet, it comes from a civilization that has been around for 7,000 years and which has seen a lot of life and living. I have no doubt that these traditional considerations and convictions steered my father's choice of my Chinese name, which means Peace, with the help of soothsayers and relatives back in China.

Besides, it sounds like winners, doesn't it? So, I'll take it! I'll take it!

* * *

The Chinese lunar calendar dates from 2637 B.C. Time is measured in full cycles of sixty years, broken again into simple cycles of twelve years each.

The Lord Buddha is said to have summoned an assembly of animals before he would depart from the earth. It was to be a race, and legend records the order in which the animals arrived.

The Rat had hitched a ride aboard the plodding Ox, only to jump off and dash across the finish line first. Thus, each year of the twelve-year cycle is presided over by a different animal in this order: Rat, Ox, Tiger, Rabbit, Dragon, Snake, Horse, Sheep, Monkey, Rooster, Dog and Boar.

In a given year, this is the animal in all its elaborately delineated traits which hides in your heart and influences your behavior.

You may wonder why the Cat isn't among the twelve. Well, true to form, the Rat had lied to the Cat as to the correct date of the race. So the Cat missed the competition. To this day, the revengeful Cat chases and catches the Rat.

In Me the Twain Have Met

Oh, East is East, and West is West, and never the twain shall meet,
Till Earth and Sky stand presently at God's great Judgment Seat.
— Rudyard Kipling

Begging your pardon, Sir Mr. Kipling, but I think you're wrong. I'm convinced that I and thousands of others like me, overseas-born Chinese, are the happy and lucky meeting of East and West. We have access to and are the product of the best of two worlds.

I was born in the frontier town of Phoenix in 1927, fifteen years after Arizona's admission into the Union. Both my mother and father were Chinese, father from China and mother American-born. I am No. 4 of nine children who survived.

At age fifty-seven, during a sabbatical year, my lifelong hope of setting foot on the land of my forefathers finally happened. What I offer here is not a journal of my city by city tour. I leave that kind of reporting to the colorful skills of *The National Geographic* and the scores of China books and periodicals flooding the market.

This is a series of reflections on the Chinese people and nation, and how I have a growing awareness of the roots of my attitudes, beliefs and values.

No one, of course, chooses his origins. We can only accept the reality of our ancestors, be they pirates and criminals or heroes and saints. An innate curiosity and a hint of fear stir deep within: who are my forebears? What were they like? Because to know them is to know myself.

I'm amused and amazed as I recall how we kids in Chinese school took it for granted that the Chinese did things first and the best way, and that all things grew bigger, better and more beautiful in China than anywhere else. Such conceit, I'm convinced, was not so much an attitude of racial superiority as simple, naive pride in one's origins.

On the trip I took along my pride and prejudice which, while often reinforced, also took a beating in light of what I saw and experienced firsthand. But above all, I found a land rapidly emerging from unspeakable pain and struggle and entering what might well be an era of phenomenal growth and long-lost tranquillity.

In the L.A. Times Travel Section I had spotted the Inter Pacific Tours International ad and its toll free 800 number. The three-week mid-September to mid-October tour was comprehensive, and July Poon, their agent, was personable and helpful. Best of all, the price was right.

I wanted to join a crowd and yet be alone, incognito. I avoided preconditioning through planning and reading, so to avoid large expectations.

An unexpected twist developed, one of many nice things to

Paul "boils in" (actually he's standing behind) one of two enormous gilded bronze cauldrons that flank the Hall of Supreme Harmony in the Forbidden City, Beijing. Death was the fate of anyone who violated the Emperor's sacred precincts.

follow. Father Paul Milanowski, a Michigan friend, listened to me outline my plans on the phone and got hooked. Just like that, he asked to come along. I was glad. He would make a fun companion. We could share room and costs, gossip about matters ecclesiastical, investigate the church's status in China and play Laurel and Hardy. The smartest thing we did was to buy a Polaroid camera and $150 worth of color film, just to take snapshots to give away and make new friends all along the way.

The other twenty-five in our group hailed from coast to coast and, luckily, proved compatible. Swapping stories, testing "anonymous" dishes for the timid, passing candies — even cough drops and other medications — brought us all closer. No lemons and spoil sports ruined the trip for all.

* * *

What's going on here? Apart from my own ethnic loyalty and curiosity, what could be the reason for a horde of 20th century "invaders" to spend so much time, money and energy to visit China? Our agency alone booked daily flights from April to November. Multiply this by all the agencies throughout the world which are handling the endless flow of the curious, the relatives, the bargain-hunters. Imagine how this strains the very limited and, by western standards, the primitive accommodations: hotels, trains, planes, buses and restaurants.

Whether by plan or accident, China has rediscovered that she is once again the center of the world. Slowly forgetting the fanatical xenophobia of Mao who fostered suspicion and hatred toward foreigners, after the humiliating years of foreign dominance and occupation, China has warily lifted her bamboo curtain.

China has discovered, too, that she is hopelessly lost without the technical tools and skills of the outside world. And she is like a bashful maiden with an incredible dowry of natural resources and precious commodities being courted by everyone.

Shrewdly, China stands happily nonaligned, even with Mother Russia, to whom she owes her Communistic ideology. She will deal with all comers on her terms. Bitter experience was her teacher.

* * *

From the next bus pulling out from the hotel, a pretty lady was waving frantically. I couldn't believe my eyes. There was Anita and daughter Lisa, two friends from Southern California.

Two wags in our group shouted back to me in the rear of the bus, "Hey, who are those beautiful dames, Emery? We're going to bust (tattle on) you!" They were teasing but they couldn't conceal their envy.

I played guilty. "Darn them! I told them not to meet me here."

In this vast land and among the millions, what are the odds of meeting someone you know?

But come to think of it, the chances aren't that slim, anymore. In fact, it will soon become fashionable to be the only one who hasn't gone to China!

Journey to My Ancestral Home

"The West can teach the East how to get a living, but the East must eventually be asked to show the West how to live."

— T. Hsieh

Departing from the Beautiful Land, Mei Kuo, our airship soared across the vast ocean to the shores of the Central Kingdom. A day had passed when our great metal bird landed in the City Up From The Sea.

By train we journeyed to the enchanting City Across The River (Hangzhou), thence to the lovely City Of Plentiful Waters (Suzhou) — being reminded of the ancient saying that "In heaven there is paradise. On earth there are Suzhou and Hangzhou."

We journeyed onward to the Southern Capital and boarded our airship again for our flight to the Northern Capital. It was there that we passed through the Gate of Heavenly Peace to behold the largest public square in the world. We strolled through the Forbidden City where the Imperial Palace remains the abiding symbol of Old China.

We hastened to the City of Western Harmony where more than 6,000 terra cotta warriors beckoned us to visit them, each one a unique and handsome face. Bidding farewell, we flew on to the City of Light And Brotherhood.

Not to be outdone, the region of Fragrant Cassia Woods called us to see for ourselves the living tapestries etched and carved in limestone by the winds and the rains along the River Li.

But my heart was set on seeing at last The Broad Region of my father and his family, origin of the world-famous cuisine that has stood for a hundred years as the standard of Chinese-American food.

Guangzhou, that is, The Broad Region, is a city of more than five million souls now, not a village any longer, nestled against the northern bank of the Pearl River Delta.

And so, as we ended our flitting-butterfly sampling of the mighty Central Kingdom in twenty-two days, we drank in the exciting beauty of The Fragrant Harbor and immersed ourselves into its teeming life.

* * *

The foregoing journey reads like a lyrical fairy tale as the proper names of places and cities are translated literally. Color it eastern.

Its factual western "translation" follows...

Hong Kong (Fragrant Harbor) will be ceded back to China by Great Britain in 1997. The modern towers of this thriving center of international trade and finance replicate the thrusting limestone peaks and formations along the River Li, for centuries the enduring image of ancient China.

China, the Central Kingdom, tried in vain to keep out invaders from the north. Begun piecemeal in the 5th century B.C. and completed in the 16th century A.D., the Great Wall snakes over 4500 miles of impossibly rugged terrain. It is a monumental architectural achievement but a colossal monument to the folly of segregation as well.

My First Trip to China

Stripped of oriental imagery, here are the facts in travel agencyese:

CHINA IN DEPTH

1984 Departure/Return Dates   B40926LN2A
Sep 26-Oct 17 Visiting 10 Cities

Day 1 U.S.A./Shanghai
Depart on Northwest Orient from Seattle for Shanghai.

Day 2 Shanghai
Arrive Shanghai; stay at modern Shanghai Hotel.

Day 3 Shanghai
See Bund, Jade Buddha Temple; Shopping.

Day 4 Shanghai/Hangzhou
Express train to Hangzhou; visit Marco Polo's "Paradise."

Day 5 Hangzhou
Cruise magical West Lake; Enjoy sightseeing.

Day 6 Hangzhou/Suzhou
Train to Suzhou and tour the classical gardens.

Day 7 Suzhou/Nanjing
Train to Nanjing on the banks of the Yangtze River. Jinling Hotel.

Day 8 Nanjing
Visit Dr. Sun Yat-sen's Memorial. Cross over the Yangtze River Bridge.

Day 9 to 12 Nanjing/Beijing
Fly to Beijing, China's Capital. Visit the Great Wall, Ming Tombs, Forbidden City, Summer Palace, Temple of Heaven, etc.

Day 13 & 14 Beijing/Xi'an
Fly to Xi'an; stay at Xi'an Hotel. See the incredible life-size terra cotta warriors.

Day 15 & 16 Xi'an/Kunming
Fly to lovely Kunming. Discover the towering Stone Forest. Visit Shi Lin Village, a commune hamlet of the Hami people, one of 55 national minorities.

Day 17 Kunming/Guilin
Fly to Guilin whose natural scenery of lakes, crags and stone towers have stood for China's landscape in art.

Day 18 Guilin/Guangzhou
Cruise and dine aboard a river boat along the River Li. See the panoramas of spectacular scenery. A short evening flight to Guangzhou's White Swan Hotel.

Day 19 Guangzhou/Hong Kong
Tour the city's highlights before departing by train to dazzling Hong Kong.

Day 20 to 22 Hong Kong
Stay at the splendid Furama Hotel. Ride up to Victoria Peak, Repulse Bay, Aberdeen. Shop in one of the world's busiest markets. Enjoy a gala farewell dinner. Depart for U.S.A. via Tokyo.

China: The Mythical Land

Sinanthropus *Pekingensis* is young. These earliest protohuman remains found in China are only 20,000 years old. He's just a kid who grew up in Asia. My roots reach across the thousands of miles from that continent.

Until 1274 when Marco Polo arrived from Venice and remained for seventeen years, China, the second largest country in the world and the most populous, lay like a huge maple leaf (nearly 3,700,000 square miles in area) whose stem is the Yellow Sea. Mongolia sits astride the upper portion of the leaf, shaped like a giant's bite, serving as a buffer between Russia and China.

Since 2,000 B.C., a unique and fairly uniform culture has spread throughout most of the country, even though, without the unifying force of a centralized government, an incredible linguistic and ethnologic diversity developed randomly.

Historically, the China Story is like the repeat of a familiar refrain: the rise and fall of dynasties and political regimes, a period of oppression with the gutting of the common welfare and, finally, with a mighty upheaval, the convulsive overthrow of a regime.

For two hundred years before Christ and two hundred years after his death, China was basking in the peaceable and progressive reign of the Han dynasty. This was the imperial age when art and literature flowered, iron tools and irrigation advanced agriculture, and trade, even with faraway Rome, bustled along the Silk Road.

Gradually, the China border formed its maple leaf shape as its far-flung boundaries stretched to embrace the towering Himalayas of Tibet, the steamy jungles of Indochina to the south and the wide open grasslands and steppes of Inner Mongolia to the north. For almost two thousand years, in spite of wave after wave of invaders, whether Mongols, Manchus or Europeans, right up to the present, the country has survived, intact.

In the earliest and bloodiest days of the Communist takeover, when our missionaries fled for their safety, Fr. Fabian proudly prophesied to me, "Don't you worry. China will simply swallow up Communism, just as a ladle disappears into a bowl of batter, and life will go on. And then we'll go back."

The Han dynasty bequeathed its name to the ethnic Chinese who make up over 90% of all the people. But while Han is their common name, they speak hundreds of different languages or dialects that are mutually unintelligible. Even Cantonese, which our family spoke, is broken into many dialects which sound like alien tongues. But, amazingly, these same millions who can't speak intelligibly to one another share the same ideograms or written words.

You will often see a frustrated traveler tracing a word with an index finger on his palm and then holding his blank palm up for "reading" by another. Then, sure enough, comes the vigorous nodding, knowing, "Hi-yah, hi-yah!".

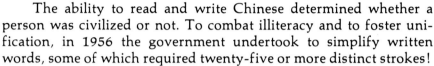

The ability to read and write Chinese determined whether a person was civilized or not. To combat illiteracy and to foster unification, in 1956 the government undertook to simplify written words, some of which required twenty-five or more distinct strokes!

Pinyin, literally "spell-sound," is a system of spelling Chinese words (sounds) in Latin letters, using Beijing (Peking) pronunciation as a model.

Putonghua, meaning Common Language, sometimes mistakenly called Mandarin, is now the official spoken Chinese language taught in all schools and used in authoritative communications.

China calls herself The Central Kingdom, probably because for thousands of years she existed in splendid isolation. She must have felt all the more so when she found herself assailed on all sides by rapacious invaders. China has lain like a gigantic oyster holding within herself a most exquisite treasure which violent, greedy thieves continually try to plunder.

For protection, the Great Wall of China was begun in 500 B.C. and completed some three hundred years later. Three thousand men slaved for ten years to link up the various segments snaking over 4500 miles of rugged mountains or, as the crow flies, 1500 miles. Its brick and stone could girdle the earth with an eight-foot high dike. Astronauts can see it from outer space. The Wall's roadway is wide enough to allow a brace of five horses and wagons to rush arms, soldiers and food to strategic defense points.

Marco Polo's fantastic journal of his experiences in Cathay inflamed the imaginations — and the greed — of all of Europe for generations. Missionaries set out to convert the "heathen" to Christ. In the sixteenth century, the first Portuguese sailed into Canton to do business, followed soon by Spaniards, Dutch and English.

In short order, the United States, Japan, Germany, Russia and France seated themselves around the table to get their share of the China pie by virtue of the "Open Door Policy." This was the euphemism used by western powers to give themselves equal commercial, industrial and residential rights and so perpetuate their high-handed domination of China's sovereign territory and trade.

The Foreign Devils had lived up to their name: foisting opium onto the Chinese, despite the government's attempts to halt its sale and use; seizing prime lands and merchandise; discriminating against the people in their own land — (signs posted in some public parks read: ENTRANCE FORBIDDEN TO CHINESE AND DOGS); operating sweat shops with slave labor; the looting of the Empress' Summer Palace, temples and monuments and invaluable art treasures.

As school children, we heard the gruesome torture stories of missionaries. What we never heard was why the Boxer Rebellion ("The Fists of Right and Harmony") happened.

The impression we were given was that the Chinese were a barbaric, heathen nation incapable of sensitivity and compassion, totally hostile to outsiders.

The truth is that this rebellion was the volcanic eruption of a

—PAUL KUO—

15

For centuries the River Li has been a paradise for painters and poets. The farmers and fishermen seem to be living figures painted against an ethereal backdrop.

17

people driven beyond the limits of endurance by the unscrupulous crimes committed against them by foreign imperialists.

The 20th century has seen the death of the dynasties, the birth of the republic under Dr. Sun Yat-sen, China's George Washington, — the bitter struggle for control between the Nationalists under Chiang Kai-shek and the Communists under Mao Tse-tung. It has even witnessed the united effort of these archenemies to expel their common enemy, Japan, which had invaded the China mainland in the name of the emperor.

Finally, in the spring of 1949, the Nationalist government escaped to Taiwan.

On October 1, 1949, a million deaths and a river of blood later, Mao Tse-tung proclaimed the birth of The Peoples Republic of China in the Square of Heavenly Peace (Tian-anmen) in Beijing.

But that's not the way it was supposed to happen!

For as long as I can remember, I've been conditioned to condemn the evil Communist system and ideal. We grew up as loyal Nationalists and sang (in Chinese) "I love the Kuomintang (Republic of China)" with the cribbed melody from "My Country 'tis of Thee" in Chinese school. We saluted the red, white and blue Nationalist flag. We listened jubilantly to the inflated news reports of Reds killed by the Flying Tigers and American aid. Our parents held patriotic fund raisers to support the freedom fighters.

And our hopes were dashed as we saw the heroic Nationalists scurry to safety across the Straits of Formosa.

October 1, 1984 — Beijing

On our TV screen in the hotel room, the scenes are of unbounded joy and celebration. It's the 35th birthday of the Peoples Republic of China. The Square of Heavenly Peace, the largest in the world, is jammed from edge to edge with a million people. The night sky is bright as midday, filled with bursting showers of exploding fireworks.

At each end of the square are enormous portraits of Mao Tse-tung and Sun Yat-sen. Premier Zhao, elder statesman Deng Xiaoping and the entire Central Committee are on the reviewing stand. Passing by is an endless parade of tanks and troops, huge, colorful dragons (symbol of prosperity), waving, proud returning Olympic heroes, Young Pioneers with their bright red neckerchiefs, carrying banners with rousing slogans.

Along the streets in every city, banners proclaiming National Day, colored balloons dancing in the sky, masses of yellow mums and fiery-red salvia plants, streets hung with lanterns in every conceivable shape: rocket ships, pandas and pagodas. In the street circles, huge dragons and cutout cranes beside pine trees signifying longevity. Giant standup characters in Chinese proclaiming: THE WORLD BELONGS TO THE PEOPLE.

I pondered then and I continue to wonder: Is it real?

For their sake — for the happiness of my people who have suffered so much and struggled for so long — I pray and hope that it is as good as it looks.

Tian' anmen (Gate of Heavenly Peace) opens symbolically onto the Square of Heavenly Peace, the largest public square in the world, capable of holding a million people. In imperial days, only the emperor, the Son of Heaven, could pass through the central gate. Today the gate symbolizes China's openness to the world and the future. Huge portraits of the "patron saints" of the birth of the republic and the Communist revolution: Sun Yat-sen, Mao Tse-tung, Marx and Lenin remind the people of their heritage.

*"Above there is heaven; on earth
there are Hangzhou and Souzhou —
and their placid West Lake."*

Where Two Rivers Joined

"You don't know how lucky you are to have had such a holy grandmother," growled this brown-robed man towering over me in the third grade. Father Martin, Franciscan friar, gruff but soft, was paying tribute to my maternal grandmother whom I had never met. He was our pastor, and when he knew your grades from the report cards he was handing out as well as everything about your family, it tended to bring out the best in you.

Grandma Sing was a saintly woman who reminded everybody of the Gospel widow who "haunted" the temple daily. She loved the church and spent hours there in intimate prayer and general tidying. She was buried in the Franciscan brown robe as a Third Order member.

Chinese-American Catholics are still something of a rarity today, particularly in the southwest. There's reason to believe that, because mother and her family spoke Spanish fluently and served Mexican dishes regularly, Grandma Sing and her family had emigrated from China through Mexico in search of gold, silver and prosperity. Without a doubt, however, the greatest treasure they found and brought to the United States was their religious faith.

It was by this roundabout route then that the Catholic faith became a part of our heritage. And for mother, named Snow Flower, the daughter of someone reputedly a saint, it was a singular blessing to claim a son a priest and a daughter a religious sister (Patricia — Elegant Moon). But her greatest joy and challenge consisted in rearing all her children in an abiding love for their faith.

* * *

My father was only twenty-three when he arrived in America, the Beautiful Land, in search of prosperity. One day he would return to his native land a successful man, a hero returning from America the Beautiful.

But then, America has not always been beautiful and certainly not hospitable.

In those days, the prosperous and aloof Chinese were harassed, slaughtered or driven from Mexico out of hatred and resentment. Some sought refuge in the United States, joining many of their countrymen who had preceded them here as coolies to reclaim swamplands or to lay the beds for the Southern Pacific railroad.

But the "chinks" met similar hostility everywhere. Civil rights were denied them; restrictive covenants barred them from living where they chose; owning property was prohibited; intermarrying with non-Chinese was forbidden.

As kids we were not allowed to use the pool at the park. We were very small when we heard "Ching-chong Chinaman, sitting on a fence, trying to make a dollar out of fifteen cents."

The sickness of prejudice was a fact of life we were taught very early.

21

This treatment has led a modern day Jew who left Brooklyn to become a citizen of the Peoples Republic of China (Sidney Shapiro who wrote "Jews in Old China") to declare: "I find an enormous similarity between the Chinese people and the Jewish people. The Chinese people have been known as the Jews of the Orient for many, many years. And with good reason, because they were discriminated against in other countries, lived in virtual ghettoes, were limited in the types of productive endeavors in which they could engage, and quotas were set for them in schools, etc...."

Imagine then the enormous evolutionary progress implied when, in 1977, Tom (Just Heart), the eldest son of immigrant Shing (Constant Abundance) Tang was confirmed for life as a Federal Judge of the United States by President Carter.

At the Senate committee confirmation hearing, responding to an invitation to express his feelings, Judge Tang asked rhetorically, "What's a Chinaman doing here? When my father came to this country, the Chinese enjoyed no civil rights. Now, within a single generation, I am being invested with the authority to interpret the laws of the land."

Father died in 1954, succumbing at last to diabetic ravages which stole away his sight and strength, despite his faithful downing of an array of evil-smelling herbal medicines.

Newspaper editorials wrote about this "Unlikely Product of the American Melting Pot" whose "engaging simplicity and generosity made his debtors grateful." He was known as a wise businessman who loved his work, compulsively perhaps, but who dispensed his munificence with an open hand that seldom closed.

* * *

Siggie, a fellow friar, has tried many ways to psych me out at golf.

"They say it takes one Armenian to undo two Jews, but it takes only one Chinaman to undo three Armenians," he quipped once as we were handicapping.

"Ah, so," I countered in my best mock Chinese. "They call us Orientals inscrutable. You know what means 'inscrutable'?"

"No, what?" he played along.

"Not able to be scruted, of course, white devil."

* * *

Father converted to Catholicism when he married mother. That is to say, he was ritually baptized and fulfilled his duties, but he had brought to his faith his many native traits which Christians strive to attain.

But he wasn't tickled when I, his No.2 son, decided at age twelve to enter the seminary. After all, what did a mere boy know about a life choice? Beneath his displeasure lay the real reason:

Chinese sons were heaven-sent blessings which meant more descendants that would bear the family name. Since Catholic priests could not marry, it made no sense to encourage such foolishness.

In the dozen years that followed, gentle dad never blocked my plans but did, now and then, hopefully suggest alternatives: why not be a lawyer, a doctor, an engineer — something that spoke of prestige?

* * *

Baptized Christians receive names of patron saints whose virtues we might emulate. I confess that Saint Richard never became my personal hero-friend-model. Who was he, anyway?

Then, consider the unseemly paradox of "dumping" one's patron saint when entering religious life, thereby symbolically discarding "the old man" and putting on "the new person" or identity.

At our religious investiture as novice Franciscans, the provincial superior removed my suit coat and ceremonially threw it out the sacristy door, while dramatically announcing: "Until now you were known as Richard. From now on you shall be called — (at this awesome moment, relatives and friends craned their necks and strained their ears to catch the new name by which they would henceforth know their sacrificial lamb) — EMERY!"

Outside later, my father approached the provincial superior and complained playfully, "Why do you want to call my boy a girl's name?"

"Girl's name? What do you mean, Mr. Tang?" asked the puzzled superior.

"Well, now you want to call him EMILY!"

As everyone knows, rich and blind Chinese continually confuse people when they talk about their cataracts and Cadillacs.

* * *

Father's mild rebuke might have meant that, in view of my choosing to become a religious, his personal choice of my Chinese name would have been more appropriate and meaningful. He had called me "PEACE," which doesn't translate idiomatically well. Western names, after all, don't carry meanings. And that's too bad. My Chinese name has spoken to me often in my lifetime.

* * *

In pre-Communist times, each Chinese village honored the namegiver/soothsayer who picked suitable and colorful names for newborn babies. Consulting astrological charts and sifting through characters from classical poetry and literature, boys were named by traits that told of intelligence and filial piety; girls by beauty and femininity.

After the Communist takeover in 1949 and throughout the disastrous anti-intellectualism of the Cultural Revolution, babies' names took on the shrillness of revolution and patriotism. For example, "Jianguo" means "Birth of the State," "Jun" means "Army" and "Ying" means "Hero."

* * *

June 10, 1945, the day Richard (Peace), son of Shing (Constant Abundance), became "Emery," a newly-invested Franciscan novice. Old Mission San Miguel, California

By 1952, broken by diabetes, his wholesale grocery business washed up and his eyes blind, Father could suddenly see. While all his obsessive working might have seemed a failure — (it really wasn't, because he succeeded in providing handsomely for his family) — he had left a legacy of kindness and generosity, gifts that would not diminish nor be forgotten.

Yet, what was probably his outstanding mistake stemmed from his Chinese convictions. For that reason he is the more easily understood and forgiven. He left nothing in his will to his five daughters.

After all, their lucky husbands would have the privilege of caring for them someday!

But such a custom never envisioned the possibility that, as happened in actuality, only one of the five would marry.

More than thirty years after his death, this costly oversight would prove to be the source of endless challenge and struggle for his descendants. Seeking personal as well as family security, both the married and the unmarried sons and daughters are forced to grapple with the tension between equality and the real needs of their own dependents.

* * *

I mark father's death by its nearness to my ordination date, June 8, 1952. That momentous day, which loomed so large in the lives of my family and my own life, was also his grandest day. He was very proud of me, he said.

Deprived now of the health and wealth he sought so eagerly in life, he saw more clearly the values he genuinely prized and which he recognized were symbolized in priesthood.

He had come full circle. The script was nearly too perfect. From one who had first resisted the idea of my ordination, he was now the first to receive its blessing.

Constant Abundance, my father, was the first person on whom I conferred the sacramental Last Anointing. He was the first one I ever buried. The date was September 13, 1954.

Here was his son, whom he had named Wo Ping, Peace, now consigning him to his Father and Maker to rest in everlasting peace.

* * *

Father was especially proud of the prayer on my ordination card, the so-called Peace Prayer of Saint Francis, rendered in both English and classical Chinese.

Wherever I went in China, I passed out copies to people I encountered. Bellhops and stewardesses, guides and waitresses, the young and the elderly — they would always read it reflectively, nodding approvingly. I loved to watch the light in their eyes as they smiled their thanks for its beauty and wisdom.

聖方濟和平禱詞

求主使我為一和平使者。在仇恨之中，
傳播仁愛；在殘害之中，宣傳忠恕；在
猜疑之中，伸述信賴；在失望之中，給
於期望；在黑暗之中，給於光明；在悲
愴之中，給於安慰。

求我恩主，使我安慰人勝於受安慰；諒
解人勝於受諒解；友愛人勝於受友愛；
因為，施惠者方能受施惠；忠恕者方能
得忠恕；死亡時獲享永生。

方濟會士　　鄧和平

EMERY RICHARD TANG
Franciscan Priest
Ordination, June 8, 1952

LORD

MAKE ME AN INSTRUMENT OF YOUR PEACE ✠

Where there is hatred / let me bring LOVE
where there is injury / PARDON
where there is doubt / FAITH
where there is despair / HOPE
where there is darkness / LIGHT
and where there is sadness / JOY ✠

O DIVINE MASTER

Grant that I may not
so much seek to be consoled as to console
to be understood as to understand
to be loved as to love ✠
For it is in giving that we receive
it is in pardoning that we are pardoned
and it is in dying that we are born
to ETERNAL LIFE ✠

ST. FRANCIS OF ASSISI

Those "Different" Chinese Kids

When I was five, still in knee pants, I trudged every day to a makeshift classroom in an apartment complex owned by my father. An attractive Chinese lady teacher — replaced later by pock-faced Mr. Yee — greeted me and my older brothers, sisters and cousins. Together we were an Asian Dozen reading, writing and struggling — to assimilate the rudiments of Chinese.

Later on, in a larger place, with the arrival in Phoenix of other Chinese families, as many as a hundred banded together and imported teachers to ground their offspring in basic skills. We concentrated on fluent reading, brush calligraphy and graceful composition in Chinese.

Chinese school ran every day from 5:00 p.m. to 8:30 p.m. and on Saturdays from 9:00 a.m. to 4:00 p.m. Summertime, except for two of the hottest weeks in July, followed the same all-day Saturday schedule every day.

Homework for St. Mary's, our American parochial school, was done at father's wholesale grocery and dry goods warehouse on Jackson Street, a few blocks from the Chinese school. What we didn't finish we completed at home around 9:00 p.m., sprawled on the living room carpet, after late dinner served by mother.

Our Chinese school teachers didn't spare the rod, literally, and woe to the kid who was out of line. Welts across our legs where the teacher flailed us with his *sah hang* (an all-purpose pointer made of a flexible vine soaked nightly in water) proved he really meant business. I don't recall a case of a doting parent defending his kid against a teacher's severity.

Not for nothing did our parents make sacrifices to hire these old country masters to shape their kids and imbue them with their Chinese heritage and virtues.

* * *

"Latchkey kids" is typical media jargon which describes the current domestic crisis in America and elsewhere in the western world. These are the students who return from school to a parentless house, since both mother and father are working. Sometimes the kids are even expected to prepare dinner for parents who get home after five o'clock.

Meanwhile, there are the horror stories about the goings-on in the parentless homes: playing with drugs and narcotics, sex games and assorted wild pastimes.

The Tang Family
Christmas 1943

Mother Father Margaret   Tom Dick
               Mary Robert
                        Rose Marie
                          Eugene
                           Patsy
                            Alice

Snow Flower

Snow Flower, our mother, stunned us all on May 28, 1980, thirteen days after her 84th birthday. She had been a widow for twenty-six years. She was made of tough stuff, remained stubbornly independent to the end, endured hearing and memory loss patiently, complained somewhat about the arthritic pain in her knee and insisted on cooking holiday meals for as many as twenty.

On her last day, she collapsed before noon and passed away that evening.

On June 4, 1980, The Arizona Republic, one of two Phoenix newspapers, carried the following editorial:

THE ARIZONA REPUBLIC

Wednesday, June 4, 1980

Chinese Matriarch

LUCY SING was the first Chinese child born in Arizona. Her father was in the grocery business in Tempe. He moved to Phoenix when Lucy was three years old. She married Shing Tang, who came to Phoenix from Canton in 1910. This accident of birth made Lucy Yee Sing Tang an American citizen. But there was no accident in the way she reared a family to take full advantage of the opportunities afforded by the American melting pot. Her nine children include:

• Tom, a Phoenix judge serving on the Ninth U.S. Circuit Court of Appeals.

• Mary, an artist and musician.

• Margaret, manager of the Social Security office in San Mateo, California.

• Emery, a Franciscan priest in Los Angeles who has played a major role in his Order's educational and television apostolate.

• Alice, a teacher at Our Lady of Perpetual Help in Scottsdale.

• Robert, an audio specialist.

• Rose Marie, a former teacher.

• Eugene, a banker in Seattle.

• Patricia, a religious sister who is a choral director and musician-singer in California.

Lucy Tang died in Phoenix at 84. Someone asked the children the secret of their mother's success. The answer was instant and unanimous: "Discipline."

In an era when family ties are disintegrating, Lucy Tang leaves the legacy of a great lady who put her children ahead of everything.

Hers is the modern version of the ancient story, told by Seneca, of the Roman matriarch who proudly displayed her diamonds and rubies to Cornelia.

When her children came home from school Cornelia said, "These are my jewels."

Snowflower, Lucy Yee Sing Tang 1896-1980.

"When we will love each other as a flower loves
— by giving freely of its fragrant self — ,
there will be everlasting peace."

— Chinese Saying

I celebrated the jubilant Mass of the Resurrection with mother's admirers who filled St. Agnes parish church where she had spent so many hours. My parting words — getting words out that morning was one of the toughest things I've ever done, but I'm glad I did — were, in effect, that Constant Abundance and Snow Flower were having one heck of a reunion in heaven, at long last.

The building reverberated as her friends sang their farewell with the schmaltzy but lovely "Santa Lucia," Lucy's favorite song.

The Children! The Children!
— Anna in "The King and I"

Children are China's obsession — and her richest resource. Everywhere one goes, the little ones are being cuddled, carried in the arms or papooses by fathers more often than is seen in the western world, receiving sweets from cooing, indulgent strangers, and posing gladly in front of any cameras.

The children's clothes are western, bright and colorful. Their jet black hair is intertwined with gay ribbons. There's a marked contrast between the cute outfits of the young and the usually drab garments of the grownups.

But what is most remarkable is that, no matter how strange the stranger, the little kids waved and smiled. They seemed fearless. They're China's heart-melting greeters. Whether standing on the roadsides or being held aloft by proud parents, the children made that close-fingered "come-on" gesture that means hi! as we passed on the street or rode past in our elegant touring bus.

This friendliness was a far cry from the chase-out-the-foreign-devils attitude of the past.

* * *

Our guide, Mrs. Lu, learned that Paul and I were priests. Young and attractive, she didn't seem like a government agent who would monitor the movement of tourists, a paranoid idea that had been planted in our heads.

I had given her a Peace Prayer card. She then revealed confidentially that her family had once been Catholics. In fact, her uncle had been a priest but was now married and living with his family in Taiwan.

Commenting on the prayer, she said in a somewhat scoffing tone, "My uncle always writes me things like that." Pausing slightly, she went on, disguising her hope with a cloak of skepticism, "Do you really believe that there is a God who moves things around here on earth? That's silly. I don't believe in that."

The more she talked to us there in the rear of the bus, the clearer it became that she was harboring a resentment against a power or fate greater than she.

In a half dozen years of marriage, she and her sportswriter husband had not been able to have a child — her deepest desire.

* * *

We visited the famous Children's Palaces, those delightful places where the kids were bussed after school. Like Catholic school children, they were all in uniform, blue and white outfits accented with the bright red neckerchiefs of "Young Pioneers" of the new Republic.

Busload followed busload disgorging tourists who climbed stairs and roamed freely through the old rundown buildings,

31

pausing to take in a whole range of varied activities.

Some children were playing western and eastern music and instruments, while others practiced martial arts, gymnastics and ballet dancing. The more technical poked around in television sets and computers, while young artists honed their skills at embroidery and Chinese brush writing.

The largest group of all was the chorus of about seventy-five pre-teen youngsters, sitting or standing in disciplined rows, like birds on wires. They were rehearsing — or were they actually entertaining? — "Red River Valley," "O, Susanna," and "Twinkle, Twinkle, Little Star" in "English," I'm guessing.

In spite of the incessant intrusions of visitors coming and going, the classes continued relentlessly. The children never stopped to gawk back at their visitors.

No one flinched as I moved about taking flash pictures. Their eyes were riveted on their old music master who sat on a stool, hunched over his podium, talking gently and firmly, coaxing precision and expression out of them. He seemed fatherly, infinitely patient and oh, ever so tired.

Those almond-shaped eyes and winsome faces were shining and animated and their voices were like chirrupy birds. But there was an unreal quality to the whole experience. It was too tidy, too perfect. The soloists' voices were pure and heavenly. But I wondered how many times they had sung these same numbers over and over again.

More importantly, I wondered what would happen if any child dared step out of line.

Or was I unconsciously reading their situation through western eyes, convinced that young people will not behave and learn unless threatened or traumatized? Is there some eastern secret to be learned here?

* * *

They're spoiled, these one-per-family angels. And grownups worry about it.

But how can this be helped, since these children have no siblings to curb and challenge them? Brothers and sisters have been denied them.

And now they are coddled and pampered by parents whose whole existence and hopes are built upon the success and failure of their lone offspring.

How will these brother- and sister-less children shoulder their responsibilities when, as adults, it will be their turn to bear the full inverted-pyramid weight of their parents, grandparents and the extended family of a whole nation?

PAUL KUO

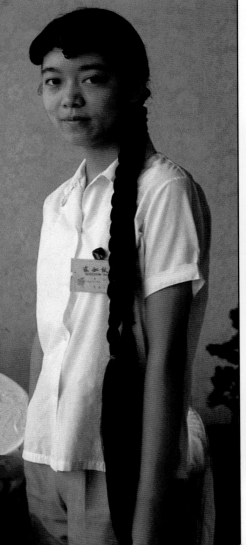

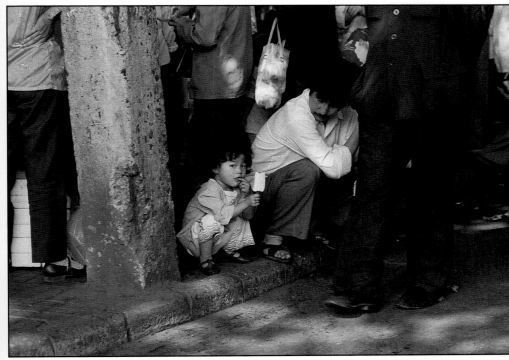

"I am not my brother's keeper.
I am my brother's sister."

"Society at large is the extended family
of mankind. All people are brothers
and sisters."

Reality Therapy

Responsible maturity is the ability to face reality and to cope with it the best way one can devise. Solving problems makes up the bulk of life's search, and the diversity of methods used by cultures is fascinating. In Christian morality the end does not justify the means, and yet the hard reality of a given situation has often forced whole peoples to adopt harsh and strange solutions to grave problems.

* * *

China's population is one billion, one hundred million — one of every four humans alive on the earth. That is the reality. The problem: how to feed and to provide for this enormous family of people adequately.

* * *

Let's imagine a boat built for a dozen persons now has twice that many, with the same number clinging to the sides, pulling and pushing to get into the boat, threatening to swamp and sink it. What to do? Would you pry loose the hands of the clinging desperate or even (God help us!) smash their fingers to save yourself in the boat?

* * *

What China did in 1979 was thoroughly pragmatic, and yet her policy would demand of her people a discipline and cooperation of the highest caliber.

Ask (or was it demand?) that a whole generation pledge to make an enormous social sacrifice: have no more than one child per family. This would reverse the phenomenal growth rate which was DOUBLING every thirty-five years and move toward a zero population growth rate by the year 2000.

Those who so sacrificed were rewarded with job advancement, free housing, education and health benefits.

Those who chose not to cooperate lost their government subsidies for health care, education, housing and pay raises. They would be forced to refund their benefits and brought down on themselves the scorn of an outraged community. Official and self-appointed snoops and tattlers exposed violators. After all, in fairness and equality, what is good for all ought to be good for every one.

Officially, coercion is prohibited. Laws clearly state that infanticide, mandatory birth control or forced abortion are serious crimes.

With all of this, the one child per family policy versus the world average of 3.2 children per family, by the year 2000 China still will have added to her population the same number of persons as live in the United States!

So much for the policy and mechanics of curbing population growth. Of much deeper significance are the long-term repercussions among a people whose whole traditional focus has been home- and family-centeredness.

Chinese society has always been family-oriented. The individual is primarily a member of a larger whole. Individualism is secondary to the good and well-being of one's family and the families of others. Family is a fundamental biological and natural structure, not a man-made construct.

Society at large is the extended family of mankind. "All people are brothers and sisters."

* * *

From my earliest awareness, I've been a Han person, Chinese, one of the more than one billion on the earth. China, however, is the home of more than sixty million (six percent of the total population) whose language, customs, religion, race and historical development make them different from the Han peoples. Officially, they are known as the National Minorities.

"They're not bound by the one child per family rule," our guide told us.

"Why is that?" asked one of the group, puzzled and, I suspect, objecting.

There was a reflective pause. Then, quite simply, he said, "Because they are minorities."

I'd wager anything that this kind of answer would never be heard anywhere else in defense of minorities.

* * *

For seven thousand years, this vast collection of peoples has kept the world's oldest civilization alive. Ripley's "Believe It Or Not" says that this number could march ten abreast to the moon and back and never come to an end — or something like that.

True or not, you tend to believe it — and then some — when you venture out in any of China's major cities. I could readily understand the westerners' chagrin: all orientals look alike.

All day, every day, you watch the ebbing and flowing seas of black, bobbing heads moving down the streets — all the streets: the main roads and the thoroughfares, the side streets and the back alleys. They come at you; they go from you. And all the while you can't help but wonder who they are, what are their hopes, where are they going, what makes their lives worth living.

There is a certain sameness among them, not so much in their facial traits, but in their stolid look and unpretentious gait. Their unexciting garb seems even to mute the atmosphere. In Communism, equality has meant the same ill-fitting olive drab and navy blue pants and jackets for men and women, topped by the red-starred Mao cap.

As I write this, I'm reminded that we religious have used the very same rationale in donning identical habits and religious garb to

Fifty-five national minorities make up six percent (sixty million) of China's total population. They differ from the Han majority in race, religion, historical development, language and customs. The one-child-per-family rule of population control does not apply to them "because they are minorities."

38

39

A bus bullies its way through the crowded streets of a village. In her race toward modernization, China faces an insurmountable task of adapting such narrow passages to accommodate vehicular traffic.

signify the poverty of common life and equality.

And yet, the signs of a coming spring are everywhere.

Young ladies, in spite of the equalizing process of two decades, remain what they have been and are: feminine.

Bicycles, the major means of transportation — there is no way possible for cars to pass through the streets of most Chinese cities — outnumber the people in the United States. The use of bicycles, however backward or primitive, has proven to be healthful. You don't see fat people. And elegance in motion is the sight of straight-back young women, hair streaming, prettily dressed, wearing inch-and-a-half heels, skillfully pedaling through traffic.

We saw teen girls wielding rakes and hoes over rocks and gravel for a road bed and were jarred by the sight. But it was softened to see that they wore dainty, dangling earrings. Beyond a certain point, equality is irrelevant.

"Oh, wow!" said Dan, half sighing, half yearning. "I just can't get over how beautiful the women are!" Dan was one of a couple of the younger set on our tour, twenty-five-ish and a vibrant, balancing presence among us. He was handsomely bearded and intensely observant.

I asked him what he meant, since he had said similar things several times earlier.

"I'm not sure," he mused. "They don't use any makeup at all and they wear very much the same clothes. I think it's their naturalness. They don't put on airs. They're so pure."

Now, how's that from someone of this generation? And I'd have to agree with him. The years of privation and the stripping away of ease and luxury have exposed the reality beneath and burnished it beautifully.

In Hong Kong we all noticed a striking contrast in the living habits and attitudes of the men and women. It would be exaggerated to say that H.K. people were spoiled, and yet it would be accurate to say that they were worldly and exotic, less "up front" and more sophisticated. H.K. teens were uncouth and loud, much like their western cousins.

Hong Kong people are intensely "westernized," in that word's positive and progressive sense, but, regrettably, also in its most unflattering, self-serving and greedy connotations.

Freedom and sophistication are not unmixed blessings.

40

Life: A Problem To Be Solved

Today was an ordinary day, but Tian'anmen Square in Beijing was filled with milling thousands of students, militia (they're easily confused with the ordinary folk attired in Mao caps and suits) and tourists from East and West who had gathered to view the body of Mao Tse-tung. It lies in Memorial Hall in a crystal sarcophagus, spotlighted, surrounded by potted pines signifying longevity, frozen and placid in form and expression, its own Long March halted.

I tried to think of what might have been the thoughts of those thousands who filed past, four abreast, silent and reverent. For their lives had all been radically affected by the spirit of the person whose remains lay there.

* * *

"It matters not that the cat is white or black, so long as it catches mice," Deng Xiao-ping has said.

* * *

Thus, if anything is necessary to lift the crushing burdens from the backs of the people, do it.

Are the birds eating the grain and are pets taking the food that ought to feed the hungry? Then kill them. Are the rich responsible for depriving the starving, oppressed poor? Then take away their property and distribute it equally. Are not all people equal? Then give them equal shares of the land that belongs to them. Are the children too great a burden on the land's resources? Then limit them. Are the foreign devils guilty of imposing hateful, foreign ways on the Chinese? Then throw them out.

* * *

Pope John Paul II's Christmas message, 1984, indicted atheism as the chief cause of "the permanent nuclear threat in the world...human exploitation...the loss of values...the scourge of famine... etc."

Outraged atheists countered with valid questions of their own: "Is it atheism that is responsible for the internecine madness in Ireland and the Middle East?

"Is it atheism that motivated the colonization of Africa and apartheid, or was it done under the pretext of bringing enlightenment and salvation to the benighted 'pagans' of the world?"

All too typically and hypocritically, commerce and profit have followed the preachers. Missioners who went "to do good" often did damn well.

"Were they atheists who assembled the atom bomb and obliterated a hundred thousand human beings? Worse yet, are they atheists who are proceeding with research into the yet more horren-

"We are the only ones who succeeded. The others had their chances but they failed."

— *Chinese Communists*

dous neutron bomb capable of vaporizing humans but, ironically, sparing their buildings?"

"Is ours an atheistic society which seems not to notice the hundreds of thousands of hungry and homeless who litter our streets?"

* * *

My Christmas mail brought messages from some Chinese acquaintances. One note was from a religious sister who, after about fifteen years of isolation from her family, was able to visit them.

She pleaded: "Please pray for my sister and my poor family. She suffers from diabetes, and the government doesn't support her needs. The people do not enjoy much freedom."

Another friend, formerly an officer with the Nationalists, now living in the U.S., wrote: "My folks suffered much...my youngest brother was executed...another was sent to land-reform camp for eighteen years. I am glad the present regime is taking another road which can lead to a better life for the Chinese people, but I cannot forget nor forgive the Communists for what they did to the people during the years 1949-1979."

A scholarly priest wrote a dissertation, part of which reads: "1400 priests and 2000 religious men and women were dispersed to work as private citizens in communes, jails or work camps. Religious education is left to parents, friends and 'barefoot catechists.' The efforts of the Holy See (Rome) to establish contacts with the government, or Communist Party, or with the Catholic Patriotic Association Church have drawn irreverent responses, misrepresenting good will as treachery. The laborious and continuous efforts have encountered great obstacles."

* * *

Our visit to China was followed by an eleven-day tour of mainland China by Cardinal Jaime Sin of Manila, himself partly of Chinese ancestry.

He was given a courteous welcome in the Patriotic churches and seminaries. But he refrained from joining with them in any religious exercises.

By not celebrating Mass or liturgy with them, he avoided the canonical "scandal of communication in sacred things" with churches separated from Rome.

So much for legalistic righteousness over courtesy.

* * *

Mother Teresa of Calcutta went to China in January, 1985. She received Communion in the Cathedral of St. Mary of the Immaculate Conception in Beijing, where we too had, only two months earlier, attended Mass and mingled with the faithful. That morning they filled the 7:30 a.m. service. I moved about freely taking pictures of the standing-room-only crowd and the mixed choir in the loft. It was my privilege to join the faithful at the Communion table.

"I was surprised to see so many people early and praying so beautifully," Mother Teresa said later, describing our own feelings

44

exactly. A parishioner who spoke English fluently and without accent had greeted us and made us feel right at home. Inside the vast church, the young and old stood reverently in the rear, quietly attentive. A mixture of staleness and sweat hung heavy. Upstairs the choir was singing polyphony.

* * *

Although the Chinese Patriotic Church was forced to split with the Vatican after the Communist takeover in 1949, Rome has always considered the sacraments of the Patriotic Church valid because they are performed by validly ordained ministers. The ministers, however, are considered unlawful because they are ordained against Vatican rules.

Mother Teresa had come to China to seek permission to establish one of her well-known hospices (her Missionaries of Charity are found in sixty-seven other countries) for the poorest of the poor.

Her request was met with an unexpected response: "What poor?"

Mother Teresa's very petition might have offended China's officialdom, since the fundamental tenet of the socialist system is to provide for the basic needs of every person without exception.

Needless to say, she was not given permission to establish her foundation.

She wrote "God bless you all" in the visitors' book of a workshop for two hundred blind and handicapped workers near Beijing.

The blind foreman responded, "We owe everything to the Communist Party."

We Visit His Excellency

"How do we get to the Catholic Church?" Paul asked Ginger, our national guide, who then asked the hotel doorman who in turn asked a cabbie. After a short huddle, the cabbie emitted a triumphant, knowing "Aaaaa!" while glancing over at us (Ginger had whispered to them that we were priests), nodding his head vigorously and slashing his hand about in a vague imitation of the sign of the cross. That was how he identified Catholics.

He would be on hand at 7:00 a.m. the next day to take us to the Cathedral of the Immaculate Conception, built in 1870, seat of the Diocese of Nanjing and residence of Bishop Joseph Qian Hui-min.

7:00 a.m. The sun had not yet risen.

Mark, our agency escort, and his petite Japanese girlfriend who was studying Chinese in Beijing came along to serve as interpreters.

The gate to the church courtyard was locked. The sexton hurried over smiling, gracious, welcoming — maybe a bit obsequiously. He led us into the dark church where only a handful of early worshippers was present for Mass. The bishop was pastor and celebrant. An older gentleman in cassock and surplice served him.

Time stood still. Barely audible, the bishop began at the foot of the altar, facing it and reciting the old Latin words: "Introibo ad altare Dei...(I will go to the altar of God)." Above, the image of the Immaculate Conception, a copy of a western holy card featuring a Caucasian madonna, looked down on the scene bathed in soft light and candles.

Out in the body of the church, the dozen worshipers knelt reverently, in no way in communication with the bishop. The sexton was leading a sing-song chant that reminded me of the auctioneer in the old Lucky Strike commercials. He was probably reciting the rosary and the people were responding rhythmically.

Thirty years ago you would have seen the exact same thing in every Catholic church all over the world.

After Mass, the bishop invited us into his reception room. Ordained — or, as their literature still refers in outdated terminology, "consecrated" — in 1981, Bishop Qian is one of fifty bishops governing 3,000,000 Catholic Christians.

The bishop was warm and gracious, very paternal, and quite willing to discuss religious matters. Only when our little Japanese non-Christian interpreter faltered over the meanings of specifically religious-theological terms did Paul and I switch into rusty "kitchen" Latin — and did quite well, thank you.

I told him I was a Franciscan friar and that this very day was, of all things, the feast of Saint Francis, October 4. His eyes lighted up and he smiled beautifully. He had just celebrated the liturgy in honor of Saint Francis, the gentle Saint of All Peoples.

The bishop clasped my hands and wished me a happy feast

Paul, Bishop Qian with his secretary-sexton, and Emery. A gift, souvenir Polaroid and tea on the feast of St. Francis.

day. I gave him and the sexton copies of my ordination card with its Chinese-English versions of the Peace Prayer of Saint Francis.

It was then that I, as described in the Prologue, asked if there were any of my Franciscan brothers still alive and well and was given an evasive no.

We drank fragrant tea, took a dozen pictures, presented him some souvenir Polaroid snapshots and left him a $100 gift.

Later, Mark confided, "I was very nervous about that money."

"Why?" I wondered. "I've been very impressed by the religious liberty and the open practice of the faith everywhere..."

"What you see is only on the surface," Mark explained. "It's highly possible that the sexton is a government spy. He might well report that gift to the authorities. There's still persecution of religion in subtle ways. Catholics meet discrimination in different ways: not getting advancements or the better jobs and so on..."

* * *

The latest "official underground" reports to the General Curia (the Franciscan headquarters in Rome which administrates the ministry of 22,000 friars worldwide) are that some forty Franciscan friars survive in China.

They enjoy a measure of "restricted freedom," all of them of advanced age, living in both the towns and rural villages.

None of them, however, communicates with persons outside of mainland China.

* * *

In June, 1985, the desecrated Beijing cathedral was rebuilt with the help of a government grant of $350,000.

Two weeks later, the Vatican declared it would loan its powerful telescope from Castel Gandolfo observatory to a Chinese university.

A month later, in July, China released from prison Bishop Ignatius Gong Pin-mei who, at 85, had already served thirty years of a life sentence for high treason: refusing to abandon his loyalty to the Holy See in Rome.

Let the thaw go on...

Benediction in Beijing's Southern Cathedral following Sunday high Mass. The altar faces the wall, the language is Latin, as though the reforms of Vatican Council II never happened.

47

Unless You Try It, You Can't Like It

MENU

Jasmine Tea	香片茶
Thousand-Year-Old Eggs	皮 蛋
Crystal Shrimp	玻璃蝦
Drunken Chicken	醉 鷄
Kidney Salad	炮腰花
Tossed Seaweed Salad	涼辨洋菜
Shark's Fin Soup	魚翅湯
Bird's Nest Soup	燕窩湯
Red Beaked Parrot & White Jade Cake (Spinach & bean curd soup)	清湯白玉板 紅嘴緑鷹哥
Deep Fried Beef Brain	炸牛膨
Braised Bear Claw with Bamboo Shoots	春芦燜態掌
Deer Tendon, Squid & Vegetables	鹿筋炒菜
Lion's Head (Pork meatballs with Chinese cabbages)	獅子頭
Three Sea Treasures (Sea cucumber, fish tripe & mushrooms)	烩三仙
Peking Duck (Served with thin pancake)	烤 鴨
Steamed Whole Fish	清蒸魚
Eight Treasures Rice Pudding (Steamed sweet rice pudding with 8 kinds of dried fruit)	八宝飯

The foregoing menu was recorded by Paul who spent hours writing notes each night before retiring. With some exceptions, it was typical of the exotic feasting on the tour.

"Don't ask Emery if it's any good," scoffed Harold. "Look at him put it away. He eats anything!" His face was twisted with disdain, distrust, distaste.

With delicious insouciance, I'd merely remark, "Look, I'm not promoting this food. Either you like it or you don't. I like it, and if you don't, there's more for me." Then I'd reach for seconds of the bony duck or chicken or sip some more tepid soup.

In the background, I overheard remarks like: "Looks like rat. Slimy. Yeccch."

When chicken isn't served up a la MacDonald's Nuggets but in cleavered, bony pieces smothered in bamboo shoots, black mushrooms and unidentifiable bits of flotsam, western novices grow queasy.

The ultimate test came when our guide explained each entree of a thirteen-course banquet. "Next there will be bees..." he announced.

"Beans?" asked someone who thought she misheard him.

"BEES," he repeated clearly.

And sure enough. There they were on a saucer, looking like elongated BB's. Just to be game, I went for it, my first taste experience with preserved bees. They were salty and acrid, not unlike biting an orange seed. For all I cared, the bees should have been left alone to collect honey, instead of being reduced to edible pellets.

* * *

The French, it is said, will eat anything once for the experience. But the Chinese will eat anything out of necessity.

China's enormous size and population, its chronic droughts and fuel shortages have contributed to the efficient method of stir-frying in large-surfaced woks. Chopsticks are best suited to the tiny, bite-sized morsels which serve more people with less. One thinly-sliced steak will feed a whole family, for example.

Religion and philosophy taught people to seek union with the natural forces in the universe. Health, pleasure and wholeness are derived from the green, growing things of earth. The joy of living is to discover nature's infinite range of sensual delights in sights, sounds, odors, textures and flavors.

Meat-and-potatoes people simply have uneducated palates. It was often the lowly peasants who first concocted mouth-watering soups and dishes from discarded animal organs, bones and entrails.

In imperial days, jaded rulers elevated the chef to the No.2 rank in the empire. The chef's task was to discover and invent ever-new taste treats for the privileged class.

Here in our country there has been a proliferation of Chinese restaurants offering Mandarin, Szechwan, Hunan and Shanghai cuisine, beyond the traditional Cantonese fare. Each style or school of cookery originated in regions that contrasted sharply in climate, product and taste.

49

Two tigers had just finished off an unfortunate coolie. As they were picking their teeth, one said sadly, "You know, we're going to be hungry again in an hour. This Chinese food just doesn't stick very long."

* * *

If we are what we eat, then our family must be half Chinese, half Mexican. And just for the record, these happen to be the No. 2 and No. 3 favorite ethnic foods in the U.S., Italian food being No. 1.

From our earliest years, our meals were prepared by one of the finest cooks who ever lived: our mother. Her meals alternated between Chinese and Mexican dishes, with plain old American grub slipped in now and then.

We always knew the joy of salsa picante, tortillas and chorizo, albondiga soup and the best tamales in the southwest.

But we also savored the (pardon the expression) tangy flavors of black bean pork ribs, delicate shark fin soup, crunchy lotus root and an endless list of oriental delights.

Mother's reputation was legendary because she seemed to be sending cakes, menudo and even whole meals over to somebody, somewhere all the time. Every Sunday was like a state dinner with at least a dozen guests. And her CARE packages helped keep me alive and happy during the war years in the seminary.

* * *

At a remote restaurant high in the mountains, I approached two Americans at a table, withdrawn from other diners. They seemed glad to converse with someone — anyone — in English.

They were from Houston, geophysicists sent by Texas Instruments to explore for petroleum. After six months of alien company and foreign diet, they were ready to call it quits.

Everything: the loneliness and lack of social life, a steady diet of strange foods, the inability to communicate with the natives — everything had conspired to make their stay unbearable.

And so it was with our group. While most were gamely manipulating their chopsticks, not many wanted to try Chinese breakfasts, have rice three times a day, drink *cha* (tea) or down local warm beer.

But I was surprised to watch how fastidiousness gave way to picking food from the common platter with their used sticks. No one seemed to mind the unsanitariness of it. And two full Chinese meals per day was a lot of chopstick practice, so that some could eventually pick up peas and even stringy vermicelli.

Three weeks was the limit for most. The sameness began to pall: same spiny carp, bony duck or chicken; the same watery soup and white rice; the same warm beer or sickly orange pop. (In L.A., there is a Chinese noodle house called SAM DAM TING.)

So a lot of food was uneaten. Waiters scraped it all into slop buckets. We were appalled at the waste in a land of so many people.

"It's not wasted," someone explained. "It will fatten the hogs."

You're One Of Us

One element distinguished me from the others in our travel group: my race. While we all came to China as tourists, I felt an affinity toward these people and an instinctive protectiveness of them and their ways.

Touring can be unintentionally demeaning and depersonalizing. The land and its people become "fair game" for oglers and the snooping eyes of cameras. Whether people washed their clothes in the river, ate their dinner on a river boat or strolled hand in hand in a park, they invariably found the curious foreigners gawking at them or aiming cameras at them, as if they were in a zoo.

But unlike anywhere else I've been, mothers and fathers seemed always willing to cooperate. Rather than shy away suspiciously, they proudly thrust their kids forward to be photographed, asking nothing for it. I have a hundred precious smiles on film to prove it.

When I saw strange and sub-standard conditions, I felt it personally. But it was worse when my fellow tourists held dishes to their noses, uttered yeccch and even pronounced them "disgusting." It was embarrassing to see phlegm spat on the streets, to enter unbearably stinking toilets or to watch children peeing on the streets through slits in their pants bottoms.

On the other hand, I was ashamed as an American of the boorishness of some in our group who ridiculed bad service, barked impolitely for tea or something else equally insignificant. There's always a tendency to expect all the world to match the level of our industrialized society or, at the very least, to understand English.

I was most proud of the unmatched Chinese custom of refusing tips for service, since foreigners are considered guests of the people. I felt humbled by the sight of these gentle people, so accustomed to suffering, satisfied with so little in the form of luxuries. Young and old, men and women and children, stood in endless lines at stores, eating places or bus lines, never shoving or scrambling for preferred places. Everyone seemed to have an occupation, no derelicts littered the streets and no beggars held their hands out for alms.

* * *

Ni Hao? Magic words. Literally, they mean, "Are you well?" "Ni hao" is the Chinese way of saying hello. The greeting never failed. If you stopped anyone anywhere and asked those words, you made a friend who rewarded you with a friendly nod and a warm smile.

I got the treatment everywhere. Thank goodness, the little Chinese I know helped me decipher the rapid fire responses: "You're one of us, aren't you?" They poked each other, stared and examined more closely this bald Han brother of theirs in western clothes, larger than they and different in manner.

"I'm a Chinese born in America, the Beautiful Land," I would answer. And then there was that look, a wide-eyed mixture of ad-

NI

HAO

51

miration, delight and maybe even envy at the good fortune of this brother of theirs. When I offered to take their pictures, they complied proudly and eagerly, arms slung across each others' shoulders. We were kindred spirits.

* * *

Our first night in Shanghai, Paul and I took a walk. It was around 10:00 p.m., just a minute too late to change our FEC (Foreign Exchange Certificates) into the People's Money of RMB (renminbi). It was a bewildering introduction to the double standard which is currently practiced in China. FECs are intended to eliminate the direct use of foreign currencies for imported items such as film, cosmetics, cigarettes and foreign publications usually obtainable in Friendship Stores. In effect, the ordinary citizen has not had access to the better grade of merchandise, since FECs are unavailable to them.

Many times we were approached by individuals with bundles of RMB, pleading to exchange them for FEC. Their urgency made them appear crooked and suspicious. Lately the police have cracked down on such solicitation.

At the hotel two pretty money changers closed their windows just as we arrived. Undaunted, we ventured out into the street which, once out of view of the hotel, was dark and nearly abandoned.

There is no traffic noise. An occasional cab may happen by, lights off (for whatever reason); bicyclists wheel past nearly silently. There is an uncanny sense of security, knowing we wouldn't be mugged or robbed.

Suddenly behind us, a man's voice asked, "Do you speak English?" We turned around to greet two young men and women. Handsome and bright, they merely wanted to practice their English, learned entirely in school or from the radio. (This kind of encounter would happen to us a dozen times. This first night's experience was a lovely introduction to this great new country.)

Their fondest hope? To visit America. Would it be possible? Not likely. But more opportunities were opening up for the younger generation and those who could save up enough money.

Paul and I came upon a snack bar filled with people of every age. Each had a pot or utensil and stood patiently in line for "potstickers" — fried dumplings being hand-formed by a crew and fried in a large wok by a head cook. The drab, greyish scene seemed lifted from a Charles Dickens novel.

"Let's go in," Paul urged. Sheepishly, we entered. All eyes were on us. Small consternation. We made feeble signs saying we wanted something to eat. Our smallest denomination of FEC not only paid for a heaping serving of dumplings and soup but also a fistful of RMB bills.

Then, presto! Like two angels, there were the two pretty money changers from the hotel. Their powder-blue uniforms stood out from all those dreary clothes of the other customers.

Alarmed, and in excellent English, one asked, "What are you

53

China is a country of many nationalities totalling one billion one hundred million people. Of these, the ethnic Chinese who comprise 94% of the total population are the Han people, a name they have retained from the Han Dynasty, China's Golden Age (206 B.C. - 220 A.D.).

doing here?! You don't belong here!"

"What do you mean, we don't belong here?"

"This is for the people," she informed us. "First of all, you should be standing in line with all those people over there. But come sit down. They've made you an exception. They'll bring you your order. Then you're supposed to bring your own spoon like we did, see?"

And she showed us the spoons they carried in their purses. "They never wash anything in these places. You could get sick from the germs."

It was a Grade D establishment, all right. Chicken bones and other detritus littered the floor. Atop the table, a cylinder of chopsticks sat, used by any and all, wiped clean but never washed. A curious but friendly crowd gathered around us. One grinning gentleman pushed the dumplings toward us, urging us to eat heartily. When the hot soup came, I felt safe from inhospitable bacteria. Paul chose to use the chopsticks. I could picture him writhing in agony later from hepatitis or worse.

Our initiation this first night passed without dire results. Our stomachs stayed calm and our hearts were warmed by this first encounter with a sincere — however unsanitary — people.

* * *

The Shanghai Hotel looms above its surroundings like a misplaced space age structure. It had been built to accommodate us foreigners. The native folk were not allowed to pass beyond its gates.

By day they stood outside the fences, peering through the bars like kids outside Disneyland. They could only wonder about the marvels of escalators and elevators, posh carpeting and elegant dining they have never experienced — or are ever likely to.

* * *

In three weeks of travel by train, bus or plane, we saw no areas we would call wasteland. Every inch of arable land that could yield something edible or useful was cultivated and planted — right up to the railroad ties our train was whizzing over.

This is all the more remarkable because we spotted only two or three tractors or bulldozers throughout the tour. Hoes and picks, shovels and rakes are still, after thousands of years, the essential tools.

It's breathtaking — and heartbreaking — to think that those endless thousands of miles of neat rows were created by the rhythmic flash and fall of hoes that we could see from our bus or train — to feed a billion mouths each day.

* * *

The lowly water buffalo, gentle and responsive as the family dog, is the nearest thing to a tractor.

Thousands of miles of terraced hills and cultivated fields are hoed and hand-watered from dawn to dusk.

58

We Proudly Present

As we are escorted through China, first by an assigned "national guide," Ginger, in our case, and then by a local guide in each city, we soon sense that our tour is carefully orchestrated. We visit attractions selected and prepared for visitors, training sites and communes where everyone is performing or working diligently, and we stay at hotels and are served at restaurants that cater only to foreigners.

It becomes uncomfortably clear that the local citizens are kept away from us and that what is provided for us is too good for them.

The pretext, of course, is that we the guests deserve only the best, but the overriding, obtrusive conviction is that we are being manipulated into believing one thing: China is not as bad off as the outside world might think.

In spite of all this public relations effort, the visitor is forced to conclude: Oh, yes, but you are — even though we deeply appreciate your efforts to impress and to please us.

We are bussed to free performances in dingy halls to marvel at fearless acrobats and elaborately costumed dancers, clever magicians and mimics who could fool birds with their whistling.

But, for the most part, the show was only a cut above the standard of a high school assembly or vaudeville. We visitors from America and Europe — I practiced my Spanish with a group of Spaniards in one of the halls — sat through the performances politely and stolidly, but when we were treated to the same bird whistling routine in different cities, it was an embarrassment. The audience snickered and clapped dutifully.

It would appear that a state school was turning out classes of birdsong-whistlers and comedians.

The dancer told a story as he hopped and twirled and beat a rat-a-tat on drums strapped to his head, shoulders and leg.

This production-line sameness permeated every factory we visited where humorless workers were making lacquered screens, weaving rugs, stringing pearls, carving ivory and jade, embroidering silks, creating lacy fans from sandalwood or nurturing flowers.

Every factory was a model of decorum, human ants at work. Never did the workers converse with visitors nor did they socialize.

"Notice that no one wears glasses, despite the very close work," our guide pointed out to us. Then she demonstrated for us the ancient, traditional method of massaging the eye area — "eight circular times on the temples in this direction, then reverse the direction, now the frontal ridge...etc." — to reduce eye strain.

Were the workers efficient and skillful? Yes. Precise and beautiful? Yes. With pride and joy? I wonder. The workers seemed like well-oiled machines. Their spirits seemed without light, even as their smiling supervisors enthusiastically rattled off their efficiency records and output statistics.

Gorgeous costumes and intricate routines by attractive actors, but lacking spontaneity.

Every factory was a model of decorum. Workers seemed like well-oiled machines; human ants at work.

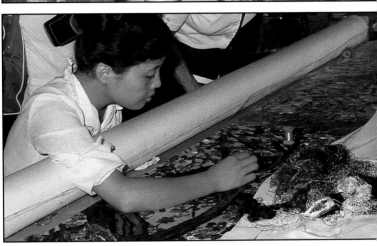

Thirty Years Behind Time

When I was a fourteen year old hot shot kid growing up in Phoenix, I was already driving the family car. No one bothered me or challenged me. That is, until a cop nabbed me and cited me on four counts: driving under age, without a license, failing to make a complete boulevard stop and speeding in a 30 mph zone.

The cop issued a summons to appear in juvenile court the next day. My sister Margaret was with me and interceded, "He's got to return to the seminary tomorrow. He doesn't have the time."

"Make time!" he snapped as he strode away. I was terrified.

By some stroke of luck I can't explain to this day, the judge called my father that evening and agreed to place me on six months probation. Easy enough, since I would be away that long in California, anyway.

* * *

In those days, the early forties, our town was host to a flood of China Air Force cadets training to fly P-51 Mustangs and P-40 Tomahawks at nearby Luke AFB. It was all very romantically gallant, associating with these dashing fly-boys of Gen. Chiang Kai-shek's armed forces who were the cream of China's crop. We idolized them. They were the guardians of the country we loved who would defend her against the Japanese invaders and the vicious Communists.

To be honest, the local Romeos were torn by patriotism and jealousy toward these uniformed poachers on Phoenix maidenhood. For, needless to say, our sisters and all the nubile young ladies of the area adored these heroes from the motherland.

As might be expected, it wasn't entirely idyllic. Reports circulated that the cadets were involved in a high number of accidents: smashed landing gears, clipped wings and assorted mishaps that were reducible to poor judgment. My sister's fiance was killed in a crash while on a training flight.

* * *

In China, only truck and cab drivers and bus operators drove. Everyone else rode bicycles or walked. Except for an occasional one-horsepower putt-putt thingamajig, the natives hauled by bikes and plowed by water buffalo.

As children in America we lived and learned how to drive cars and to operate machinery. In China only the very few have the opportunity.

Experience in China is limited; skills and intuition cannot be sharpened. How could a young man who never so much as drove a car be expected to handle a hurtling fighter at speeds in excess of 300 mph?

* * *

The local laundromat is the nearest river.

A hand-poled transport barge is a family's means of livelihood on the Grand Canal.

There are among us aliens who speak an unintelligible gobbledygook and smirk arrogantly all the while. Their speech is laced with jargon like: user interface, software base, modems, floppy disks, internal expansion, RAMS and chips.

They're computer freaks, of course, who seem to be in another world, communicating on another level. They peer into green screens and punch away on keyboards, mysteriously creating an ever-changing array of words, data and graphs.

We shake our heads in amazement, feeling lost and ignorant, wishing we could do it with the same ease.

This is the same kind of disparity and inadequacy that afflicts the Chinese, held back for thirty years, struggling to make up for lost time but who find themselves like stutterers whose tongues and lips can't keep pace with their ideas.

* * *

The glitzy hotels like the Nanjing Jinling, built by western money (probably) and know-how, will match any four-star hotel in the world. And yet, brand new and ultra-modern as the hotel is, it is frustrating to find faucets leaking and mildew covering the tile grout. Elsewhere the high-performance elevators wouldn't perform at all or were infuriatingly slow.

It's obvious that, while the attendants and bellhops were attired in spiffy costumes and uniforms, they often proved themselves to be empty packages neatly wrapped. They lacked the knowledge and the skills to maintain these technologically advanced structures and machinery. They who probably still used "honey pots" for bathrooms at home would not understand too well the principles and physics of flush toilets. Nor would they understand the power and effectiveness of chemicals for sanitation and cleaning.

The high fashion show that was held in The Great Wall Hotel in Beijing reeked of artificiality. Male and female models strutted their stuff in far-out designs that bore no resemblance whatsoever to Chinese art and style. The fashions were crude attempts to ape western styles, and the walk and manner of the mannequins lacked the finesse of their counterparts in the west. Bluntly put, the show was boring and the clothes ugly.

Change is not a matter of changing clothes or slapping on decals to mask over the past. Development and growth come about molecule by molecule, inch by inch, slowly and laboriously.

We were glad, I'm sure, to have the luxurious comforts of hotel living but we subconsciously yearned to see the ancient images of open-shirted natives slogging through the mud of a rice paddy behind water buffaloes or sampans tossing on the waves.

The romantic tourist in us secretly preferred to travel back in time to a primitive era of quaint sights and sounds, as though life were a stage.

We want to see the new — but not too fast.

How to Get Rid of an Enemy

"The best way to get rid of an enemy is to make him your friend."
— Chinese Fortune Cookie

PEARL HARBOR

"We're at war!" shouted Bob, my wide-eyed classmate. It was December 7, 1941.

We were baby freshmen at St. Anthony Seminary, Santa Barbara, five hundred miles from home and suddenly very afraid. In the ensuing months, Navy planes practiced bombing and strafing runs in the channel off the coast. At night the city was blacked out. A Japanese submarine boldly surfaced off Goleta, ten miles north, and shelled an oil tower — probably to instill a bit of psychological terror by proving they could get close without detection.

The same insolent Japanese who had been chasing Chiang Kai-shek across China had now attacked the United States. The gall of them!

Anti-Japanese sentiment exploded. All of Japanese ancestry, citizens or not, were herded into detention camps. My aunt Mary and her daughter Betty Jean were put in concentration.

Christmas vacation meant an overnight train ride to Phoenix. Father Rector prepared an affidavit attesting to my Chinese ancestry, lest I be mistaken and assaulted for being Japanese.

A glowering conductor eyed me suspiciously. "You Chinese or Japanese?" he snarled.

"Ch-ch-chinese..." I stammered, quivering.

"Lucky for you," he threatened. "You all look the same to me, and for all I know, you might be lying. My son's in the Navy, and I've vowed that, if he gets killed, I'm going to grab the first Jap I see and slit him from his belly up to his throat!"

FORTY YEARS LATER — BEIJING

Japanese tourists, hundreds of them, filled buses, hotels and restaurants. These young and old were descendants of an ancient enemy whose blood once soaked the ground on which they walked now.

They sat impassively at tables and ate meals that were not as tidy and artistic as theirs would be. And I couldn't help wondering what thoughts passed through their minds as they recalled the young sons, brothers and lovers who gave their lives for a fanatical cause on this land.

WELCOME, YOUNG JAPANESE FRIENDS

Scarlet banners stretched across Beijing streets with that warm greeting. Three thousand young Japanese were flown from Tokyo as guests of the Chinese government to attend a Sino-Japanese Friendship Convocation.

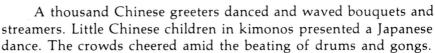

A thousand Chinese greeters danced and waved bouquets and streamers. Little Chinese children in kimonos presented a Japanese dance. The crowds cheered amid the beating of drums and gongs.

Two weeks later, it was time for the young visitors to return home to Japan. The farewell scenes on television were heartbreaking. Tears flowed freely as the young people clung to each other not wanting to go.

How right the wise Fortune Cookie!

* * *

I once had a favorite student in a high school where I served as principal. A day came when, due to familiarity, she overstepped her bounds. I reprimanded her. Stunned, she retreated.

Later, she presented me a card which read: "Time wounds all heels." Who could resist that?

* * *

Time, the Great Healer.

Twenty years ago, in the mid-sixties, the rabid Red Guards, unleashed by Chairman Mao, literally torched the nation. To bring a faltering revolution back on course, Mao had whipped the youth into a frenzy of reaction against counter-revolutionaries and rightists who would water down the purity of the Communist gospel.

They beat and tortured and slaughtered a hundred thousand intellectuals, teachers and merchants. They burned books, defaced temples and churches, and destroyed cultural relics.

Inflamed by revolutionary rhetoric, they tried to re-live the glorious marches of the Red Army of the thirties and forties that had saved China from a thousand evils.

When Chairman Mao died in 1976, the Cultural Revolution died with him. Disenchantment has set in like dry rot. Even the master's teachings are questioned.

Now in their thirties and forties, the Red Guards find themselves uneducated and unskilled. Whereas they should be today's leaders, they watch helplessly as their younger brothers and sisters stride past them or leapfrog over them.

These are Mao's Orphans, his Lost Generation, despised and rejected by the survivors of their cruelty.

Today, China seeks harmony.

Officially, her leaders exonerate the hated Red Guards. "If these young people in their teens and early twenties did something wrong, the main blame should not be placed on them."

The government encourages night courses to educate and rehabilitate them and sponsors social events designed to reinstate them into the mainstream of the community.

It is another Long March toward forgiveness and acceptance.

Rest in Peace

Grandpa Tang was brought over from China by his son, my father. Only now, forty years later, can I reflect adequately on what it must have meant for him to leave behind his beloved land in a flight to safety and freedom.

He arrived, frail and scarcely able to walk, assisted by his wife, father's stepmother. All day he sat in a living room chair, silent, lost in his thoughts and memories, safe from threats to his life but uprooted and severed from his life's threads.

He died in his mid-nineties, a few years after arriving. Father Donohoe, our pastor and family friend, administered a belated baptism and last anointing and gave Grandpa Tang the Christian name of Joseph.

The funeral at St. Agnes was a circus. A large crowd of Chinese folk filled the building, chattering all the while, wholly unfamiliar with the Latin and English goings-on.

The funeral cortege could have been the longest in Phoenix memory. The end car was out of sight of the lead hearse. We children couldn't believe it. While most of the sympathizers had never met the old man, they were at his funeral in deference to his elderly satus.

After the graveside rite, our family climbed into the limousine to leave. Suddenly, several men approached the grave with joss sticks and packages which they arranged around the grave.

My father was obviously embarrassed by this clash of religious and cultural practices. He made a move to get out and shoo the people away. But Father Donohoe restrained him. "It's all right. Let them be," he said, reassuringly.

These gentle people had brought along foodstuffs for Grandpa's trip to the land of his ancestors. It would be a long and arduous journey, and they wished him well.

* * *

An American was joshing his Chinese friend, after they had witnessed a similar ritual at a Chinese funeral. "Why do they leave that chicken and stuff at the grave?" asked the American. "Do they expect them to come out and eat it?"

The Chinese thought a moment and replied with a question, "Why place flowers on your graves? Do you think they're coming back to smell them?"

* * *

Coping with the mystery of death is the ultimate challenge to every person and culture. While I made no special study of the Chinese method of dealing with death, we saw enough of their religious monuments to reveal general beliefs.

The vast Ming Tombs complex was tucked into foothills where the winds and waters combined (feng shui) to make it an ideal

Buddhism came to China from India in 100 A.D. But the Laughing Buddha, patron of hope, is a Chinese development, the happy evolution of Confucian and Taoist influence. Strict moral standards, rebirth and life after death were principal beliefs of Chinese religion.

Departed spirits are a horde of restless, demanding, revengeful souls who make life miserable for the living who fail to keep them happy.

resting place. For 3,000 years the Chinese rulers built their tombs in this area. They employed geomancy or divination to determine where the terrain would best shield their bodies from the evil spirits that were borne by the northern winds or where the cool, flowing waters would refresh their souls.

The roadway to the Ming Tombs is lined by mammoth, stone-carved figures: camels, lions, elephants, horses and mythical beasts, followed by haughty mandarins who were to be guardians of the emperors and their wives in the next world.

In 1620 Emperor Wan Li provided well for his two wives. Their remains lay side by side in magnificent lacquered coffins, sixty-five feet below ground. Marble thrones and stools stand ready for them, as well as jeweled crowns, solid gold chopsticks and plates. Fully outfitted, the Empress would bear about fifteen pounds of hairpins, jewels and a crown of gold and jade and other precious stones on her poor, royal head.

Today the entire area, once sacred and entry forbidden under pain of death, is a favorite tourist and picnic spot.

* * *

In China, a visitor has to force himself to appreciate artistic skill that could create so many garish and (to my taste, at least) repulsive carvings and imagery that fill the temples. Writhing, contorted, leering figures portray struggles between good and evil forces, gods and demi-gods.

Buddhism came to China from India in 100 A.D., although it quickly became in effect a native religion. Pointing to a gold-leafed, pot-bellied, grinning Buddha behind a glass case, our guide said that original Buddhism never envisioned a Laughing Buddha, patron of joy, hope and good times. Believers prayed to him in their dark moments.

Guan Yin, originally a male deity, in time was transformed into a female goddess through popular belief. She would be the Chinese counterpart to our Virgin Mary who dispensed qualities of mercy and kindness.

* * *

More than six million (!) people die each year in China. Under pain of severe penalties, the government has decreed that cremations replace most burials to save precious land.

Communism has always maintained that religion is to blame for people's superstitions and the stoic tolerance of widespread social ills. But in spite of the official stance of atheism and brutal religious persecution, the government has not succeeded in stamping out centuries-old beliefs and convictions.

* * *

In the traditional Chinese view, the natural and the supernatural are two facets of the same whole. Earthly happiness, the goal of life, is surely followed by happiness hereafter, as day follows night.

So vivid is the belief in the next life that a condemned criminal is said to have begged to be strangled rather than be beheaded, lest he enter the afterlife deformed.

But the happiness of the departed is controlled by those who still live on earth, so that communication with the dead is taken for granted.

In Christian belief, the living are taught to pray for the helpless, departed poor souls.

In Chinese belief, the departed spirits are a horde of restless, demanding, revengeful souls who can make life miserable for the living who fail to keep them happy.

Wooden ancestral tablets bearing the names of dead ancestors are enshrined in each home, candles and incense are burned, family members bow and special foods are offered before the tablets. Paper money is burned and the graves are swept clean and tidied.

Family members must constantly humor the dead through such gifts, reverence and prayers or else suffer terrible retribution in the form of sickness, poverty, failure or other misfortunes.

Ancestor worship, it turns out, is not "adoration" of the dead, as is often thought, but rather a craven fear of them.

Our guide was leading us through the temple gardens, explaining the carvings and the architecture, along with the beliefs of the worshipers. An occasional robed monk would pass by, eyes cast down, indifferent to the world.

Our group entered a temple. Some kind of service was in progress. The guide spoke through the bullhorn to reach all of us easily, quite oblivious of the ritual.

A monk was praying facing three or four sad-faced people.

"Why are they wearing those arm bands?" asked one of our group, standing not more than three feet away.

"Oh, it's a funeral going on," answered the guide, blaring rudely over the bullhorn, completely insensitive to their grief.

Communism, lest we forget, is concerned with the plight of the people here, not hereafter. The "pie-in-the-sky" of religion does not put food in the bellies of the hungry nor lift the boot of the oppressor from their backs.

In the Chinese view, earthly happiness, the goal of life, is surely followed by happiness hereafter.

China's enormous potential and dramatic emergence will fix the focus of economic as well as political power on the Pacific Basin nations.

In the mid-fifties, Chinese leaders dreamed of spanning the mile-wide swiftly flowing Yangtse River. The water separated the Beijing capital from other major cities in the Lower Yangtse River Valley, especially Shanghai and Nanjing.

The Slumbering Giant Is Stretching

The L.A. Times (March 28, 1985) reported a confession by China's Premier Zhao. "Your other leaders and I lack experience with the economic changes of the scope that China is now carrying out."

What candid honesty! We Americans are more accustomed to smokescreens or lies which make us feel secure, at least, even though we might not be. Politicians bluff and pretend they have everything under control.

In 1984 China's gross national product (GNP) swelled by 13% and her growth rate surpassed the U.S. and Russia by nearly 6%. Since adopting the "self-responsibility" of agriculture ("meet your government quota; the surplus is yours") in 1978, China has doubled her output of food grain and is now the world's largest producer of wheat and cotton.

In the urban sector, workers are to get better pay for more work and more freedom to choose jobs.

The People's Liberation Army has been reduced; military expenditure trimmed. Eighty thousand senior officers will be out to pasture by 1986.

Predictably, there has been a national binge on TV sets, washing machines, watches, refrigerators and other electrical appliances. Bank loans increased by 29% in 1984; wages rose and the money supply expanded. When one billion people (200 million households) make a run on certain commodities, they could easily tilt the balance of the richest nation's reserves overnight.

China's dramatic growth will fix the focus of economic as well as political power on the Pacific Basin nations, create strong trade pressures on the U.S. and radically affect Russia's future policies.

No wonder the Premier confessed. "We intend to keep the economy under tighter control as we proceed with our economic reform program," he said.

* * *

Items in the daily press: "Spiritual pollution (the infusion of foreign values and ideas) threatens the purity of Communist economic reforms...; authorities fear rock and pop music, disco dancing, fancy clothes and lipstick — all the rage of Chinese urban youth; reading materials should focus on healthy, positive themes. Workers should not waste their hard-earned money on street tabloids with their lurid tales of crime and sex...."

Deng Xiao-ping sounds like he is trying to harness a bucking bronco he has loosed: "The goal of our liberalization program and of socialism itself is to achieve common prosperity. Those sections of the country and those persons who become wealthy first are supposed to help the rest of the nation...If polarization develops between the rich and the poor, or between the prosperous coastal areas and the impoverished inland regions, then our program will fail."

In 1970, after a demonstration of our TeleSPOTS (religious "soft-sell" commercials produced and distributed by Franciscan Communications, Los Angeles) at the International Religious Broadcasters Convention in Tokyo, I went to Taiwan to visit friends and to arrange for airing of TeleSPOTS there.

Customs searched my luggage. The TeleSPOT film reel was suspect, even though I declared it to be religious in nature. No matter. Banned. No entry. The reel was confiscated, to be returned at departure time.

That was my introduction to Taiwan paranoia.

Since then the world has witnessed the assassination of a Chinese-language journalist in northern California by thugs of the Bamboo Gang, a Chinese mafia. It seems they were dispatched by the Taiwanese chief of military intelligence to murder someone who would dare criticize the current regime.

In other news, Taiwanese spies in China were jailed for allegedly collecting intelligence, recruiting agents and inciting defection, especially among air force pilots from the Peoples Republic of China.

In September, 1984, the widow of the late Premier Zhou En-lai pleaded with Taiwan "to give up their policy of building a wall around the island and to create a favorable atmosphere of national reconciliation....; to facilitate trade and cultural, scientific, sports and tourist exchanges and promote communication between the people of both sides of the Taiwan Straits and family reunions. To procrastinate will only increase Taiwan isolation and instability and will serve only to demoralize the people who worry about their future."

Since 1979, the Peoples Republic has offered Taiwan a plan that would make that country a special administrative region with its current social system unchanged after reunification. Taiwan would be allowed to keep its own armed forces and exercise independent jurisdiction with the right of final appeal.

* * *

In 1997, Great Britain will finally cede its rights over the territory of Hong Kong. China has agreed that the capitalist system is to be retained intact for at least fifty years.

Generous? Of course. But not entirely unselfish. Hong Kong happens to be one of the world's greatest financial trade centers. And Deng Xiao-ping knows a gold-laying goose when he sees one.

"ONE COUNTRY, TWO SYSTEMS" sounds like talking out of both sides of one's mouth. The world is waiting to see. "By adopting the open policy, China is allowing capitalism to enter. This will supplement the development of socialism and is beneficial to the development of socialism's productive forces."

YIN

YANG

Epilogue

In Chinese thinking, each person is considered to be a tiny part of the vast universe, so that one's body and spirit ought to reflect and correspond to the flow and movement of nature as a whole.

Chinese medical theory is based on a central concept of Chinese thought: that good health is the result of maintaining a complementary balance between the two great forces of Yin (陰) and Yang (陽).

Yin is perceived as relating to things female, moist, soft, dark and cold. Yang is the opposite, relating to things male, dry, hard, light, hot.

With the flow and movement in all of nature, the Yin/Yang forces are in a perpetually shifting balance or tug o'war, as it were. Sickness then is the imbalance of the Yin/Yang forces that can be righted by medicine and therapy.

Whereas in the West evil is perceived as an entity, a demon adversary to be exterminated, the Chinese think of it as something needing augmentation, affirmation and healing. Life's perpetual purpose and struggle is to center rather than to destroy.

Good and evil are twin aspects of the same reality. Peace and harmony are the healing balance between two opposing forces.

Thus, the aphorism "Thorns Have Roses" can be equivalently stated as "Roses Have Thorns."

If Yin means that today is cloudy and cold, then tomorrow's Yang or sunny, warm day cannot be far behind.

China has been through this before, many times during her 7,000 year history. Her struggle through bloody revolution and hellish purge seems nearly over, again.

China is on the verge of breaking out of her confining pupa. She is about to draw back her bamboo curtain.

No other nation has ever attempted to shed its Marxist constraints or at least to dilute its extreme measures. But already the signs are clear and unmistakable.

A new day is dawning.

Departing from Hong Kong was a shambles. Our Northwest flight was abruptly cancelled. Panic. People in the lines were pushing, shouting, angry. Mark and the local guide were running all over getting each of us on board alternate flights. Only hurried, distracted goodbyes as our group dissolved into the mass of humanity.

I was seated in a 747 jetliner, next to two young Los Angeles-bound ladies. They had just completed two weeks in China. Like two school girls, they hauled out their loot: pearls, exquisite necklaces, bracelets and rings, oohing and aahing over them, triumphant and glad they had splurged.

"Did you like your China experience?" I asked.

"Oh, god, yes!" with no if's, and's or but's.

"If you were to sum up your whole trip, what would you say was the most unforgettable thing about it?" I was curious.

Without the slightest hesitation, one said, "It's got to be the friendliness of the people."

When all is said and done, what greater compliment can be paid to a person or, even better, to a whole people?

"The most unforgettable thing about the trip was the friendliness of the people."

China is about to draw back her bamboo curtain.

謝々您来看我，再見！
THANK YOU FOR VISITING ME. GOOD BYE!
請再来
COME BACK AGAIN.